Felix Mendelssohn

COMPLETE WORKS FOR PIANOFORTE SOLO

Edited by Julius Rietz

From the Breitkopf & Härtel Complete Works Edition

In Two Volumes

Volume I

DOVER PUBLICATIONS, INC., NEW YORK

Published in Canada by General Publishing Company, Ltd., 30 Lesmill Road, Don Mills, Toronto, Ontario.

This Dover edition, first published in 1975, is an unabridged republication in two volumes of *Für Pianoforte allein*, originally published in four volumes by Breitkopf & Härtel, Leipzig, n.d., as Series 11 of *Felix Mendelssohn Bartholdy's Werke. Kritisch durchgesehene Ausgabe von Julius Rietz. Mit Genehmigung der Originalverleger* (complete edition published between 1874 and 1877).

International Standard Book Number: 0-486-23136-4
Library of Congress Catalog Card Number: 74-77285

Manufactured in the United States of America
Dover Publications, Inc.
180 Varick Street
New York, N. Y. 10014

Contents

Capriccio in F-sharp Minor, Op. 5 (1825)

Original publisher: Schlesinger'sche Buch- und Musikhandlung, Berlin.

Sonata in E Major, Op. 6 (1826)

Original publisher: Friedrich Hofmeister, Leipzig.

Allegretto con espressione.

22

Molto Allegro e vivace.

Seven Characteristic Pieces, Op. 7

Dedicated to Ludwig Berger. Original publisher: Friedrich Hofmeister, Leipzig.

1.

Sanft und mit Empfindung (Quietly, with feeling)

2.

Mit heftiger Bewegung (With violent motion)

3.

Kräftig und feurig (With strength and fire)

Allegro vivace.

4.

Schnell und beweglich (Fast and lively)

5.

Ernst und mit steigender Lebhaftigkeit (Serious, with increasing vivacity)

FUGA.

mf sempre legato

6.

Sehnsüchtig (With longing)

48

7

Leicht und luftig (Light and airy)

Presto.

*sempre staccato e **pp***

*sempre **pp***

Rondo Capriccioso in E Major, Op. 14 (1824)

Original publisher: Friedrich Schreiber, Vienna.

Fantasy on "The Last Rose of Summer," Op. 15

Original publisher: Friedrich Schreiber, Vienna.

Andante con moto.

Three Fantasies or Caprices, Op. 16 (1829)

Dedicated to Ann Taylor, Honoria Taylor and Susan Taylor, respectively. Original
publisher: Friedrich Schreiber, Vienna.

I.

SCHERZO.

II.

III.

Andante.

Fantasy in F-sharp Minor, Op. 28 (1833)

Dedicated to Ignaz Moscheles. Original publisher: N. Simrock, Berlin.

Con moto agitato.

Con moto agitato .

Andante cantabile e Presto agitato in B Major (1838)

Composed for the *Musikalisches Album* of 1839.

94 Presto agitato.

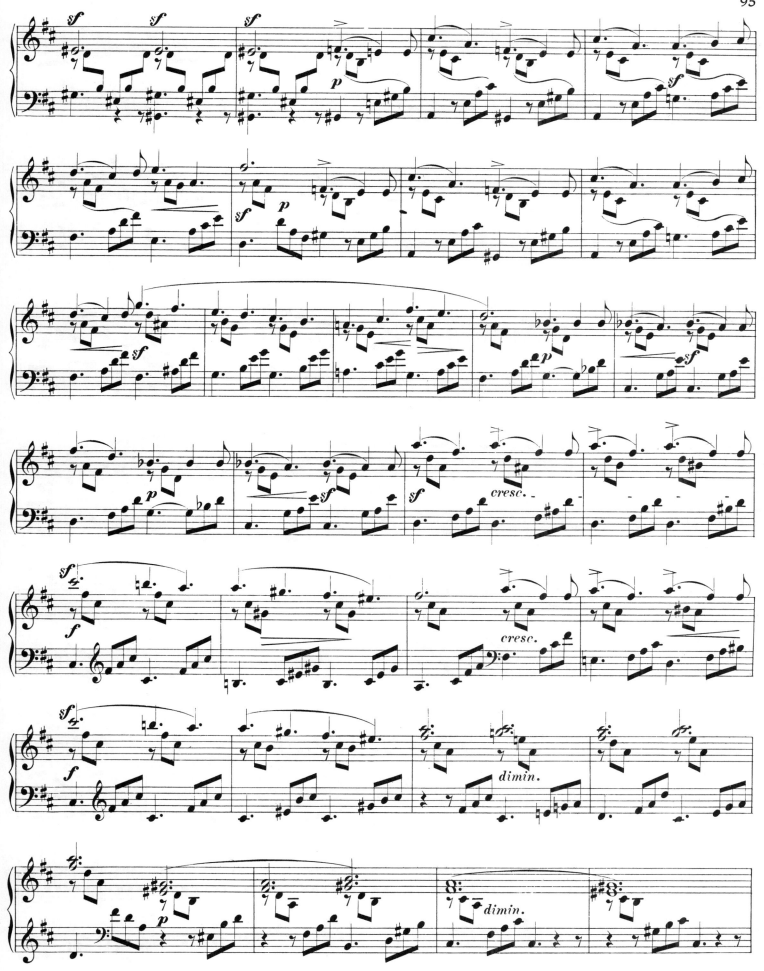

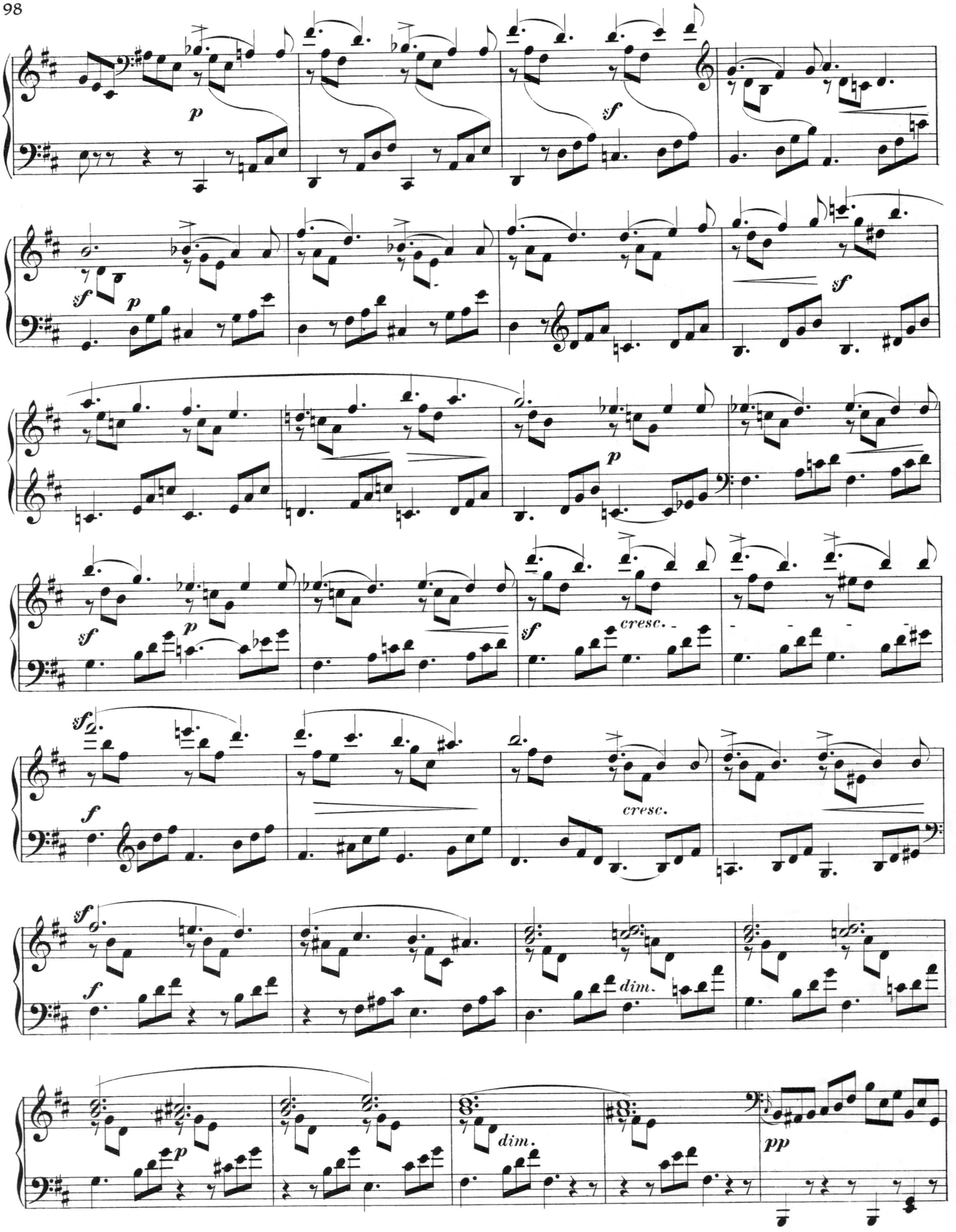
p
sf
sf
p
sf
p
sf
p
sf
cresc.
sf
f
cresc.
sf
f
dim.
p
dim.
pp

Etude in F Minor (1836)

Composed for the *Méthode des Méthodes*. Original publisher: Schlesinger'sche Buch-
und Musikhandlung, Berlin.

Scherzo in B Minor

Original publisher: Schlesinger'sche Buch- und Musikhandlung, Berlin.

Gondola Song (Gondellied) in A Major (1837)

Original publisher: F. W. Arnold, Dresden.

Scherzo a Capriccio in F-sharp Minor

Composed for the *Album des Pianistes*. Original publisher: N. Simrock, Berlin.

Presto scherzando.

Three Caprices, Op. 33 (1833-1835)

No. 1 composed 1834; No. 2, 1835; No. 3, 1833. Dedicated to Carl Klingemann.
Original publisher: Breitkopf & Härtel, Leipzig.

I.

II.

Allegro grazioso.

III.

Presto con fuoco.

Six Preludes and Fugues, Op. 35 (1827-1837)

Prelude No. 1 composed 1837; Fugue No. 1, 1827; Prelude No. 2, 1836; Fugue No. 2, 1835; Prelude No. 3, 1837; Fugue No. 3, 1832; Prelude No. 4, 1837; Fugue No. 4, 1835; Prelude No. 5, 1836; Fugue No. 5, 1834; Prelude No. 6, 1837; Fugue No. 6, 1836.
Original publisher: Breitkopf & Härtel, Leipzig.

Praeludium I.

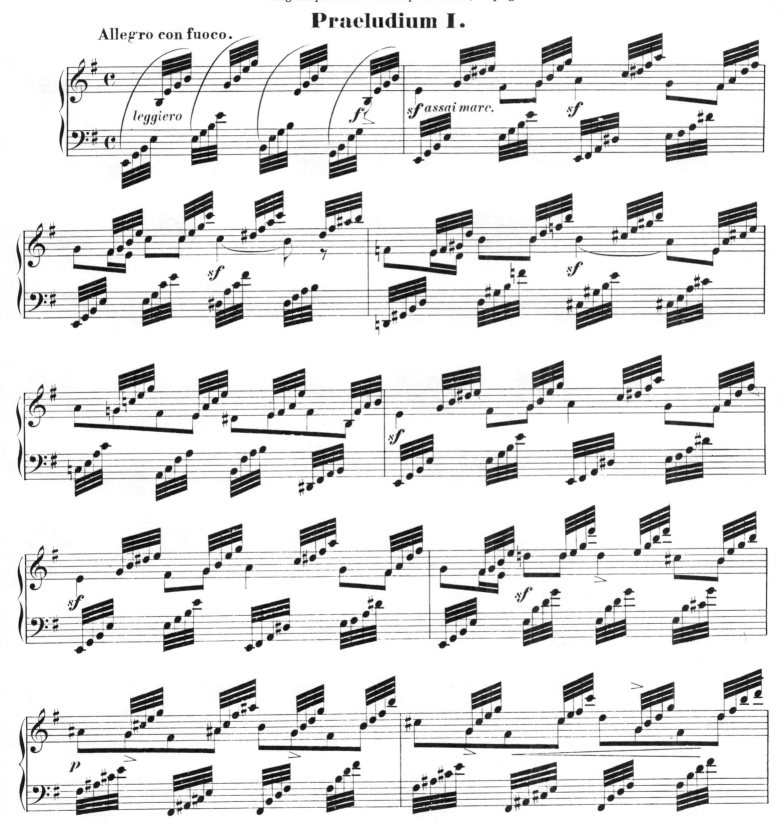

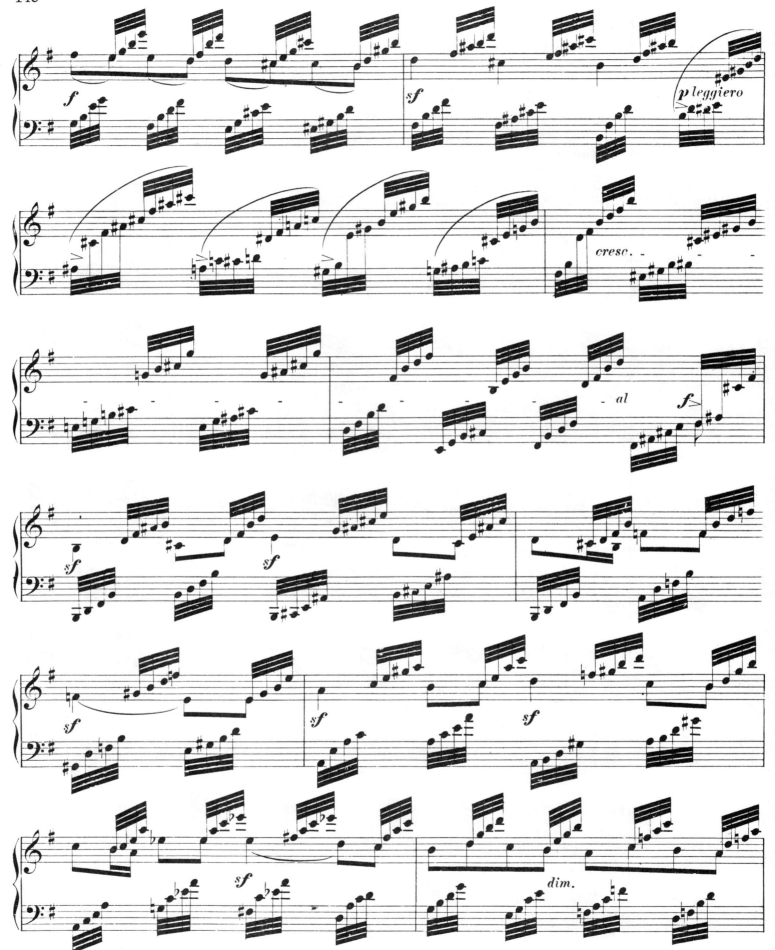

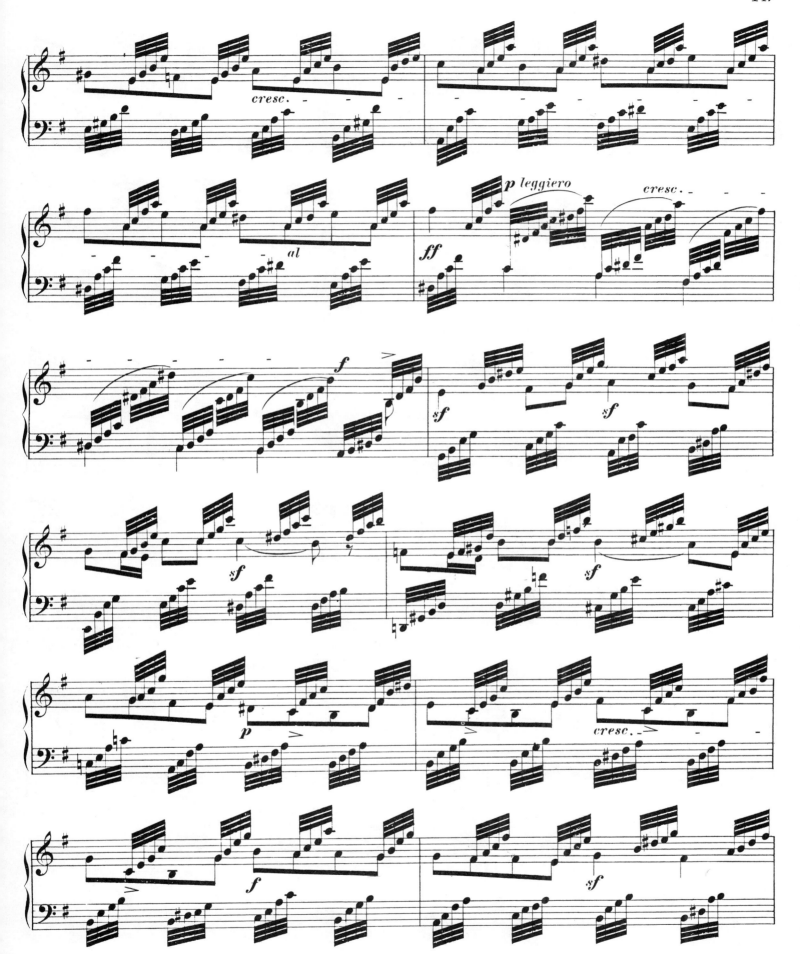

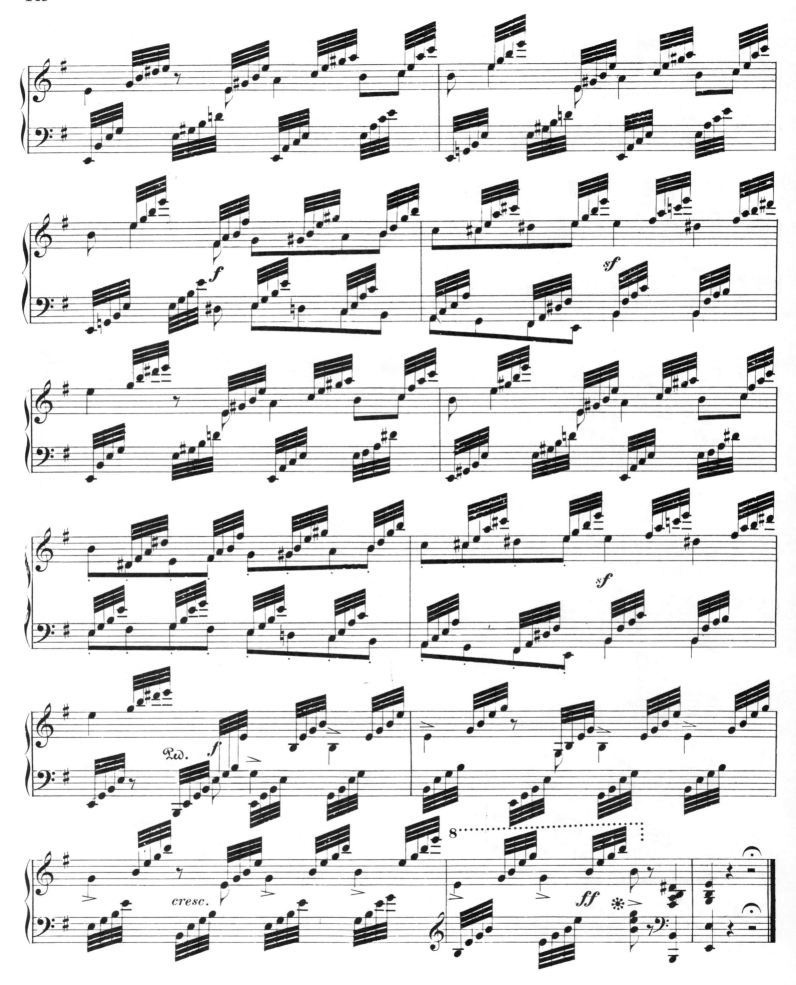

Fuga I.

Andante espressivo.

Praeludium II.

Allegretto.

Fuga II.

Tranquillo e sempre legato.

Praeludium III.

Prestissimo staccato.

Fuga III.

Allegro con brio.

Praeludium IV.

Fuga IV.

Con moto ma sostenuto.

Praeludium V.

Fuga V.

Allegro con fuoco.

Praeludium VI.

Fuga VI.

Allegro con brio.

Variations Sérieuses in D Minor, Op. 54 (1841)

Original publisher: Friedrich Schreiber, Vienna.

Var. 6.

Var. 7.

Var. 13.

sempre assai leggiero

sf sempre assai marcato

Six Pieces for Children, Op. 72 (c. 1842)

No. 1 is dated 1842 and dedicated to Lilli Benecke. No. 3 is dated 1842 and dedicated
to Eduard Benecke. Original publisher: Breitkopf & Härtel, Leipzig.

1.

2.

3.

Allegretto.

4.

Andante con moto.

5.

Allegro assai.

6.

Vivace.

Variations in E-flat Major, Op. 82 (1841)

Original publisher: Breitkopf & Härtel, Leipzig.

VAR. 5.
Tempo I.

sempre col Pedale

dimin.

✳ senza Ped.

dimin.

pp ritard.

sf   dimin.

pp

Variations in B-flat Major, Op. 83

Original publisher: Breitkopf & Härtel, Leipzig.

VAR. 2.

VAR. 3.
Allegro.